With Love
Today + for a Lifetime
Chris + Madeleine
10·6·00

MARS & VENUS
365 WAYS TO KEEP
YOUR LOVE ALIVE

MARS & VENUS

365 WAYS TO KEEP YOUR LOVE ALIVE

JOHN GRAY

MACMILLAN

Pan Macmillan Australia

First published by Random House U K, London.
All rights reserved.
Published by arrangement with Linda Michaels Limited,
International Literary Agents.
First published in Australia in 1999 in Macmillan by
Pan Macmillan Australia Pty Limited
St Martins Tower, 31 Market Street, Sydney

National Library of Australia
cataloguing-in-publication data:

Gray, John, 1951-.
Mars & Venus: 365 ways to keep your love alive.
ISBN 0 7329 0983 X.
1. Marriage. 2. Communication in marriage.
3. Interpersonal relations. I. Title.
306.872

Cover design by the Senate, London

Printed in Australia by McPherson's Printing Group

CONTENTS

LOOKING FOR LOVE

When your heart is open, you have the ability to know if someone is right for you.

When we mistakenly think men and women are the same, our relationships are filled with unrealistic expectations.

When a woman is willing to
unlock the doorway to her heart,
then men will come knocking.

Contained within the awareness
of our soul's need for love is the
intuitive knowledge and power to
find its fulfilment.

It takes a consistent and
monogamous blending of
energies to recognise a
soul mate.

Receptive feelings that attract
a man are trust, acceptance and
appreciation.

When a woman is able to face the part of herself that needs love, it is easy for a man to be attracted to her.

For a man to be attracted to a woman, he needs to feel that he can make a difference.

A man will feel his need
for a woman's love much more
than a woman will feel her need
for a man.

To open herself to love, a
woman must be receptive to
receiving support from others.

LOOKING FOR LOVE

If you are quick to fall in love,
be careful to proceed slowly and
let the relationship pass the test
of time.

When our hearts are open,
we are able to act in accordance
with our highest purpose,
which is to love.

12

When we can make decisions
from an open heart, then we are
able to create a better life.

When a man doesn't have to
worry about how difficult it will
be to get out of a relationship,
he is much more inclined
to get involved.

To ignite romantic feelings a
woman needs romantic intimacy
while a man needs physical
intimacy.

When a man is uncertain, his
approach may be to do nothing
and say nothing that could be
used against him.

To feel a soul connection
with someone our hearts
must be open.

Soul attraction is the
recognition that you have what a
person needs for his or her soul
to grow, and your partner has
what you need.

It makes a woman feel special
when a man is willing to risk
rejection to get to know her.

A woman provides the kindling
so the heat of romance can
slowly build, eventually to ignite
the bigger logs.

When a man really likes how he feels around a woman, he begins to like her more.

Flirting is very exciting to men because it complements their ability to make a woman happy.

Women enjoy it most
when a man takes the risk to
impress her rather than waiting
for her to do something
to impress him.

Instead of talking about himself,
a woman wants a man to ask
questions and be interested in
getting to know her.

A confident and competent
man is very attractive to a
woman, but what makes her
more interested in him
is his ability to ask questions
and listen.

A man instinctively doesn't
reveal his excitement, assuming
that if he appears needy it will
weaken his position.

A woman is excited by the thought of being seen, heard and desired, and reassured by the possibility of getting what she wants and needs.

A man is excited by the thought of winning a woman over and encouraged by a feeling in his gut that says, confidently, I could make her happy.

When a woman pursues
a man, automatically he will
relax more and become more
passive about the relationship.

Before sharing his vulnerable
side, a man should clearly
demonstrate that he can be
responsible for himself and
for her.

When the lower needs for
survival are met, then the higher
needs for love and intimacy
become more important.

From a man's point of view
there is a world of difference
between a needy woman and a
woman who needs him.

A woman needs:

… someone who cares about
her well-being, to understand
what she is going through and
recognise the validity of
her feelings.
… someone to love freely
and trust that she will be loved
in return.
… someone to notice her,
love her and adore her.

A man needs:

... someone to accept him
just the way he is.
... someone to trust him and
depend on him for what he
can provide.
... someone who admires him for
what he has done or tried to do.
... someone who gives him the
opportunity to fulfil her needs.

A woman needs:

... someone she can confide in,
who is trustworthy and will not
turn on her or break her
confidence by revealing her secrets.
... someone who understands
what she likes, and makes plans
so she doesn't even have to think.
... someone to anticipate her
needs, wants and wishes, and to
offer to help without having to
be asked.

Soul mates have many shared interests, but quite often they have many more different interests.

To find your soul mate, go to places where the people have different interests from yours.

Ways to meet your soul mate:

… make eye contact with the
person that you are interested in.
… at a party, when a woman
continues to move around,
a man has an easier time
approaching her.

Women are like the moon,
men are like the sun.

Receiving cards, cut flowers and little presents; moonlit nights; spontaneous decisions; and eating out all spell romance.

When a man plans a date, handles the tickets, drives the car and takes care of all the small details, that is romance.

Ideally, we must be generally fulfilled and complete before entering into an intimate relationship.

♥

As long as a man has not experienced the reality of making a woman happy, he will hold a fantasy picture.

We are most likely to find a partner when we are not desperately looking for one or depending on one to be happy.

A soul mate is not perfect, but perfect for us.

The right person for us is recognised by our soul, not by our mind.

❤

You cannot pick a soul mate by trying to figure out if they are right.

A soul mate is someone
with whom in our heart of hearts
we feel longing to share our lives.

When our soul recognises a
mate, we are not recognising
someone who is better than the
others, we are recognising
someone with whom we can grow
together in love for a lifetime.

The time for a man to begin a relationship is when his desire to give is greater than his need to receive.

Before he makes a commitment, a man must make sure he is ready to put his best foot forward and not hold back.

It is action that sweeps
a woman off her feet, but she is
not dependent on a man doing
big things.

It is no longer enough to find
someone who is willing to marry
us, we want partners who will
love us more as they get to know
us; we want to live happily
ever after.

The challenge of dating
is to find a partner who will be
supportive of our physical needs
for survival and security, and
who will also support our
emotional, mental and spiritual
needs as well.

Choose to love, not just for
yourself, but for your children,
your friends, and even the world.

The fastest way of finding a
special partner or being found by
someone is to create positive
dating experiences.

Understanding that men are from
Mars and women are from Venus
will not necessarily make any date
a lasting relationship, but it will
make dating more fun, more
comfortable and more rewarding.

Through taking the risk,
following your heart and
exploring relationships to find
the right person, you are
preparing yourself to find true
and lasting love.

When soul mates fall in love,
there is simply a recognition.

Finding the right person for you is like hitting the centre of a target. To aim and hit the centre takes a lot of practice. Some people may hit the centre right away, but most do not.

When our hearts are open, we are able to be attracted to and even fall in love with the right person.

It is as clear and simple
as recognising that the sun is
shining today, or the water you
are drinking is cool and
refreshing and the rock you are
holding is solid. When you are
with the right person,
you just know.

A man is attracted to a woman
who clearly can be pleased.

There are basically four kinds
of chemistry between partners:
physical, emotional, mental
and spiritual.

❤

Physical chemistry generates
desire. Emotional chemistry
generates affection. Mental
chemistry creates interest.
Spiritual chemistry creates love.
A soul mate has all four.

The first challenge in the
process of dating is to give up
searching for your soul mate and
instead focus on preparing
yourself so that you can
recognise your soul mate when
they appear.

Knowing who you want to
spend your life with comes from
opening your heart.

To sustain attraction, we must
express our best and most
positive self.

The more we have learned to
express freely who we are and to
feel good about ourselves, the
faster we move through the levels
of discernment.

Distance not only makes the heart grow fonder, but also gives a man the opportunity to pursue.

When a man is attracted to a woman, he gets excited because he anticipates that he can make her happy and that makes him feel really good.

A woman need never feel
obligated to please a man.

When we begin to feel that we
would really like to get to know
someone and have an exclusive
relationship, it is quite natural
suddenly to shift and not feel
so sure.

A woman becomes more
attractive when a man clearly
knows what she wants.

You cannot make someone
physically attracted to you.
All you can do is create the right
conditions to make that person
discover what chemistry
is possible.

When we feel a chemistry with
a partner on all four levels –
physical, emotional, mental and
spiritual – then we are ready
for intimacy.

When we are finally able to
recognise our soul mate, in the
beginning it is only a glimpse.

Since everything these days is
so fast, we tend to move too fast
in dating. We must be careful
not to give much more than our
partner is giving.

A woman needs to understand
what makes her special to a man.

Every relationship is a gift.
It offers us the opportunity to
prepare ourselves for finding and
recognising a soul mate.

The more discerning we become
about whom we are willing to
share a relationship with, the
closer we get to finding our
soul mate.

After a woman begins to feel
all four levels of chemistry –
mental, emotional, spiritual and then
physical – her heart begins to
open to a man.

When a woman reacts to a
man's advances, he feels more
connected to her.

When a woman is focused more on giving than receiving, when she cares more about pleasing him than about what would please her, a man will not become more interested in her.

Compliments are the best way to communicate our attraction and allow it to grow.

Choosing to date someone
for reasons that do not resonate
with our level of maturity will
sabotage our ability to move
through the five stages of dating.

A woman particularly
appreciates a compliment when it
focuses on something she has
put a lot of herself into.

When a woman flirts with a man, she is simply interacting in a manner that expresses the feeling that maybe he could be the man to make her happy.

The first few dates for a man are like presenting his résumé: 'Here I am; this is what I have done and can do. Ask me anything.'

When dating couples learn to master basic communication skills, they can experience the success, intimacy and fulfilment in their relationship that not only encourage them to move through the five stages of dating but also ensure that they continue to grow in love for a lifetime.

Most people find or are found
by their soul mates when they
are not really looking.

When a man can communicate
that he definitely likes a woman
and wants to spend more time
together, it is music to her ears.

Once you think you want an exclusive relationship, it is important to start one and see if you like it.

A man is most interested in a relationship when he feels he has something to offer and share.

By understanding the dynamics
of what makes men and women
attracted to each other, dating
can not only begin to fulfil our
need for intimacy, but can also
help us to discover and express
the best parts of who we are.

Women are most attracted
to a man who is confident.

The greatest power a man or
woman can gain to create
attraction is the ability to
awaken in another more of who
the other is.

♥

It is the feeling of being
inspired to be our best that can
make dating and relationships
so fulfilling.

For most, self-assurance needs to be developed and cultivated. It is already inside a woman; it just needs the opportunity to come out and be exercised.

A self-assured woman trusts that others care and that they want to support her. She does not feel alone.

A strong and assertive woman can be very attractive, but she must learn to express her power in a feminine way.

♥

As a woman grows in self-assurance, she will not be attracted to men who cannot respond to her in the ways she deserves.

When a woman is self-assured,
she fuels a man's confidence and
his anticipation of success.

Having a positive and open
attitude about our differences
causes men and women to be
more attractive to each other.

By focusing on sharing positive feelings on a date, a woman can ensure the natural development and unfolding of attraction in a relationship.

What makes a man most attractive to a woman is his ability to make her feel like a woman.

By being a sympathetic listener, a man can transform even a disappointing date into an intimate and rewarding experience for the woman.

By taking time to be romantic, a man gets an opportunity to experience and remember why he is doing it at all.

A man with a purpose is most attractive to a woman. When he has a plan, a dream, a direction, a vision, an interest, or a concern, he is very attractive.

A man becomes even more attractive to a woman when he focuses his purposefulness on her.

When a woman is attracted to a successful or influential man, what she is really attracted to is the responsible side of him that made him successful.

Whether intentionally or unintentionally, we put ourselves in the right place to meet a potential partner with whom we can feel immediate chemistry.

Every day, without knowing what they are doing, individuals happen to do the right thing to find a soul mate. They put themselves in the right place at the right time, and then it can miraculously happen.

Soul mates basically have similar levels of maturity.

The insight that different interests create chemistry explains why it is sometimes so hard to find a soul mate.

♥

By actively seeking out situations where people have different interests, we dramatically increase our chances of experiencing more chemistry and meeting the right person.

Whenever you go somewhere new, a new part of you has a chance to come out. One of the reasons we are attracted to people with different interests is because we are stimulated in their presence.

Soul mates basically have something that their partners need.

Emotional chemistry frees
us from being limited by our
unrealistic pictures of what our
ideal partner will look like
or be like.

We will automatically feel
a chemistry with someone who
reflects our levels of maturity
or depth.

To find a soul mate, not just a
secure partner, takes new insight,
education, and lots of practice.

Even when we feel chemistry
with someone, we can easily
make the mistake of assuming
that we are just too different to
make a relationship work.

We cannot fully recognise
a soul mate until we are ready.
We need to know ourselves
before we can recognise the
right person for us.

A man will often ignore his
feelings of attraction unless a
woman looks a certain way.

If we want to be happy and well loved for a lifetime, the wise man doesn't judge a book by its cover.

Passion can only be sustained when the attraction we feel is based on something more than just a woman's appearance.

BUILDING YOUR LOVE

When you feel really good
about your life, whoever comes
into it has to enhance it.

♥

The desire to share our lives
with someone is the expression
of our deepest soul.

Instead of feeling uncomfortable
– feeling I should do everything
and have no vulnerability –
I find I really feel loved when
I'm cared for.

When one person takes a step
to open his or her heart, it
moves us all toward greater love.

Love can last a lifetime
but it requires the ability to
continually let go of our
expectations about how our
partner should be and behave and
to find a greater understanding
and acceptance.

Men are not afraid of intimacy,
nor do they need years of therapy
— they are from Mars.

To love is the wilful intention
to serve your partner according
to his or her wishes, and an
openness to receive your
partner's support when it serves
your needs.

Commitment sometimes
helps to make peace with your
differences.

Encourage your partner to tell you
what he's thinking. If he doesn't
want to talk, don't press.

Sometimes, gentle persistence is
all that is needed to help your
partner to let go of their resistance.

For women, staying in contact
is a way to show you really care.

Give your partner permission to take care of himself and he will give you permission to take care of yourself.

Men hate being told what to do, but if you ask whether they are willing to hear things, they appreciate it.

Appreciating your man's
actions is like a secret magical
love potion; immediately he is
relieved and at peace.

It helps to remember that it is
not your partner's responsibility
to be the sole provider of
everything in your life.

What we get out of a
relationship has more to do with
what we give, than who the
person is.

A man thrives when he feels
that he is successful in being
there for others.

A woman primarily needs to be loved for who she is, rather than what she does.

T aking time to be alone allows a man to feel his independence, self-sufficiency and autonomy.

In a love relationship, we replace
our need for love with the need
for our partner's love.

Finding true and lasting love
doesn't mean we will be able to
feel it all the time. Everything in
the world moves in cycles.

When we can express the best
of who we are, we gradually
create the good fortune to attract
in our lives all the opportunities
we need.

A woman is the jewel and a
man provides the right setting
for her to shine.

On Mars there is a
very strong belief and instinctive
tendency not to deviate from a
formula that works.

We cannot create chemistry
but we can either prevent or
support its growth.

M ost women have not yet
learned the art of being assertive
and feminine.

S elf-assurance means
you will always get what you need
and you are now in the process
of getting it.

A man will most respect and want to hear what a woman has to say when she speaks in a manner that assumes he wants to hear what she has to say.

A receptive woman is able to receive what she gets and not resent getting less.

A woman's responsiveness is
most attractive when it is
authentic and not exaggerated.

It is not so much what a woman
does that makes him happy but
the way she responds.

A woman does not want a man
to give up his goals in life in
order to make her happy.

Instead of not helping at all,
a man needs to realise that
sometimes the best way to help is
just to be there for her.

Romantic rituals are there to make a woman feel special and to remind her to receive and not to give so much.

By sharing, a woman is able to release the burden of feeling solely responsible.

Instead of needing a man primarily for survival and security, a woman needs a man for emotional comfort and nurturing.

Resonance of values creates a basis from which we can work through our differences and find fair compromises.

We are attracted to someone who is different in order to satisfy the deep yearning of our soul to expand and embrace that which is beyond ourselves.

As we love our partners over time we actually start becoming more interested in their interests.

A great sex life is not just the symptom of a passionate relationship, but is also a major factor in creating it.

A man feels free to try new things when he knows he can always come back to the tried and true.

Every woman is different.
For a man to truly understand
what she needs, a simple
discussion at some point can
make a big and lasting
difference.

A woman's responses to a man's
touch give him all the feedback
he needs.

A woman wants to be teased or gradually led to the place where she is longing to be touched.

When a man takes responsibility to take care of things, he allows the woman to relax and enjoy being taken care of.

When there is someone to greet
us at the end of the day,
someone who recognises our
worth and benefits from our
existence, it gives our life
meaning and purpose.

We are our happiest
when we are loving.

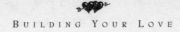
As we grow in love, we naturally become more dependent on our partner for love.

The love we share is not always idyllic, but the hope of being loved will still buffer us from the cold, uncaring, indifferent world outside the relationship.

Instead of feeling powerless to
do anything, remember and
honour your loved one.

W e are happiest when someone
cares for us, makes us feel special
and important, understands our
sorrows, and celebrates our
successes.

When we have a strong sense of
who we are, we can bond with
another without losing a healthy
sense of our worth.

What a woman needs today
in a relationship is a man who
will respect her feelings.

By listening and containing his feelings, a man can build his masculine power to make his partner feel more feminine.

What children need most is for their mother to be fulfilled.

By creating a balance between
love and work, a man's chances
of finding success and keeping
that success go up dramatically.

A balanced life is like a magnet
that will draw in opportunities
for greater success.

The foundation of a loving
relationship assists a man greatly
in being able to accomplish
his goals.

♥

A man thrives when he feels
that he is successful in being
there for others.

By giving in the right measure, a man doesn't have to hold back from giving, but instead gives what he can and gets the appreciation he needs.

When our hearts are open, we can be assured that we are getting closer to our goal.

With a heart full of love, you will express your highest potential while also fulfilling your soul's deepest purpose: to love and be loved.

Always remember that your love is needed.

A soul mate is someone who has the unique ability to bring out the best in us.

When our relationships make sense to us, we don't make as many mistakes.

Even in the best relationship
there is room for growth.

Physical attraction can be
sustained for a lifetime only
when it springs from chemistry
of the mind, heart and soul
as well.

To fully receive love, a man needs to experience that the love he receives is the result of his efforts and achievement, not just because he is a good and loving person.

A women loves nothing more than a note, showing that she is always being thought of...

On the level of the soul, you are the same throughout your life. You are you all of your life. The soul is that part of you that doesn't change.

The soul is that aspect of who we are that is most lasting.

Once we begin to get our emotional needs met in a relationship, our hearts begin to open and we experience real love and intimacy.

When our soul wants to marry our partner, it feels like a promise that we came into this world to keep.

As we become more autonomous and mature, we automatically begin looking for more in our relationships.

Soul mates are not perfect, but when your heart is open and you know them, they are somehow perfect for you.

The love you spontaneously feel
for a soul mate is the foundation
for learning to share your life
with someone who in many ways
is very different from you.

Ultimately, taking the time
to really get to know someone
is the secret of success.

After getting to know our
best sides, we are ready to deal
with the less positive sides of
who we are.

After being receptive to a man's
advances and appreciating his
efforts, a woman doesn't owe a
man anything.

When a woman falls in love,
she may feel as if she is already
getting everything she could
ever want.

A man's doubts are dispelled,
not primarily by what a woman
does for him, but by how she
responds to what he does for her.

A man automatically looks at a
relationship like an investment.
He puts his energy in and hopes
to get something out of it.

When a man's physical desire
is also the expression of his love
for a woman, then this is the
best time to experience
increasing degrees of intimacy.

A man's heart has a chance to
open fully as he experiences
increasing physical intimacy.

When the right person comes
along, you just know. And you
spend the rest of your life
discovering why he or she
is the right person.

When we are able to feel and
experience the best in ourselves
and in our partners, we are then
ready to experience all of them and
allow them to experience
all of us.

After expressing positive responses
becomes an automatic habit, a
woman is ready to move into the
intimacy stage of a relationship.

Spiritual chemistry gives us the power to overcome the judgements, doubts, demands and criticism we may sometimes experience.

When our hearts are open and we love, respect and appreciate our partners, we are capable of supporting them even when they are not as perfect as we might have thought in earlier stages.

As a woman slowly opens up to experiencing more intimacy she has a chance to rise up in waves of increasing fulfilment and pleasure.

For many men it comes as a surprise when they experience that mental and emotional intimacy can be as fulfilling as physical intimacy.

When a man experiences his
partner without the stresses of
marriage, but with the clear
recognition that he wants to share
his life with her, he is able to feel
his most confident, purposeful
and responsible self.

Each partner needs to experience
that they have the power to give
of themselves and be successful.

Each time we act and react
in a manner that will keep the
commitment of the soul, we
once again open our hearts and
align ourselves with our
highest purpose.

When a relationship is giving a
woman everything she wants,
she is motivated to make it
even better.

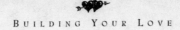

There is something special about every woman, but what makes a woman more special to a particular man is the special chemistry he feels for her.

Through finding the gift or the good in each relationship, we will eventually make our dreams come true.

When you have seen the best of a person, your heart has a chance to open. With enough love in your heart, you are prepared to experience the worst in that person and still come back to a loving connection.

A man thrives when a woman is open and receptive to his interest and his attempts to interest, impress and fulfil her.

As her love grows, a woman is able to discern whether a man is right for her, not because of his ability to be the perfect partner, but because in herself she feels an unconditional love that recognises, 'This is the person I am here to be with.'

A woman gives what she would want and assumes it will make a man most interested in her.

A woman is most fulfilled
when her needs are met, while a
man is fulfilled primarily
through being successful in
fulfilling her.

A woman mistakenly thinks
that to be worthy of receiving
what she really wants, she must
keep giving back what she is
receiving.

Desire, interest and passion
in a relationship come from
dynamic tension. This dynamic
tension is created, awakened, or
'turned on' when a man gives
and a woman receives graciously.

A man forms an emotional
bond of affection as he succeeds
in making a woman happy.

The direct way to a man's heart
is through complimenting and
appreciating the things he
provides.

When a man receives from a
woman, it opens him up to
receive more, but when a woman
receives from a man, it opens her
up to give more.

When a woman expresses her feminine radiance, she is generally embodying the three basic characteristics of femininity: she is self-assured, receptive and responsive.

Receptivity is the ability to benefit or find something good in every situation.

When a man expresses his masculine presence he is generally embodying three basic characteristics of masculinity: he is confident, purposeful and responsible.

A man will most respect and want to hear what a woman has to say when she speaks in a manner that first assumes he is interested.

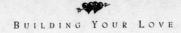

With new experiences of love
and friendship to hold on to in
present time, it is easier to let go
of our past.

Although there is nothing
wrong with a woman expressing
her masculine attributes, it will
backfire if she doesn't also get a
chance to sometimes be
feminine.

When a woman behaves and interacts with a man – assuming that she will get the respect she deserves, that she can get the support she needs, and that she is already worthy of that support – then automatically she brings out the best in him.

The secret to being responsive is to be authentic.

A man loves it when a
woman feels free to be herself
in his presence.
He is turned on by her ease and
comfort with herself and her
freedom of expression. When she
can be herself in his presence,
that is a message to him that he
doesn't have to change
to be with her.

A woman can sense
when a man is confident.
She automatically begins to relax
and feel assured that she will get
what she needs.

♥

Accepting a man while
disagreeing with him makes him
feel free to be different.

Confidence in a man makes a woman breathe deeper, relax, and open up to receive the support he has to offer.

A confident attitude reassures a woman that everything will be all right.

Accept that it's OK to think differently about money, children, sex, work, spending time together and so on... you're just from different planets.

Understand that giving love is different for every one of us, and then you will understand how to be with each other.

Women love a man with a plan. A woman doesn't like it when a man is too dependent on her for direction.

A man needs to have a sense of purpose separate from his relationship.

When a man is self-directed
and self-motivated, a woman feels
very relaxed and comfortable
with him.
Rather than feeling she needs to
take care of him, she feels he
has the energy and motivation to
take care of her sometimes,
and for her this is good.

For a man to stay on purpose
in his relationships, he needs to
remember why he is having a
relationship anyway.

Even if a man is not
responsible in all areas of his life,
his ability to be passionately
purposeful and responsible to
what is most important to him
will always show.

A woman's self-assurance that she can and will get what she needs makes her most attractive and prevents her from feeling needy or desperate.

Soul mates have similar values that resonate.

When we are with our partner, what is most important to him or her resonates with what is really important to us.

When a woman is receptive to what he is offering, a man gets the message that he may be accepted and not rejected.

It is wise to first know yourself before trying to share yourself in marriage.

A marriage proposal should be a free and joyful expression of our heart's desire.

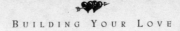
The love we feel when we are engaged is not only real and lasting, but also infused with hope. It is like a seed that contains the vision of possibilities for our future. It is the foundation on which we will build our lives. To nurture that seed and give it a chance to grow, we must take the time to celebrate our love.

Being engaged provides
a strong and necessary
foundation for taking on the
challenges of moving in and
sharing the complexities of life
with your partner.

The engagement stage is
an opportunity for a couple to
create lasting memories of their
special love for each other.

A woman will be more successful in marriage by remembering the clear and loving feelings she experienced while being engaged.

During an engagement, you have the greatest ability to learn and practice the two most important skills of staying married; the ability to apologise and the ability to forgive.

Marriage is the acknowledgement that our partner is special to us on all levels and that we are committed to the growth of love in the relationship.

By keeping our promise to love and cherish our partner above all else, we are able to open our hearts again and again.

Keeping a sense of humour,
a sharp memory of your differences
and a commitment not to take life
so seriously are the keys to a
healthy and happy marriage.

The odds for succeeding in
marriage are actually very good:
imagine if fifty per cent of the
people who go to Vegas
won the jackpot.

By keeping our soul's promise, we infuse our lives with meaning, grace and purpose. Marriage is the acknowledgement of that promise, and making sure a marriage works is the fulfilment of one of our soul's highest purposes.

By making the commitment to get married, we automatically strengthen and support the recognition that we love this person so much that we want to spend the rest of our life with him or her.

When we are happy and healthy in our relationship we can be good parents.

Instead of playing down
our love and affection, we should
deliberately express it in front of
our children.

One of the greatest challenges
of single parenting is continuing
to nurture your own adult needs.

TROUBLES IN LOVE

If we try to clearly see our partner's loving intention, our relationships automatically change. Instead of feeling rejected or unappreciated, we see the love that was always there.

Everyone makes mistakes. To forgive those mistakes is the action of love.

When we understand that men are from Mars and women are from Venus, we see that the other is not being obstinate, stubborn, or disagreeable, but is just from another planet.

When you give hugs within a couple of minutes you can dissolve away all of the hurt and anger.

Sharing values makes us compatible with someone. It helps us to overcome the challenges that come with any relationship.

When we focus on forgiving what is easiest, then gradually our ability to forgive is strengthened so we are capable of forgiving the big ones.

To apologise is to say that you understand and validate your partner's response, and acknowledge you made a mistake you intend to correct.

A woman's greatest challenge is to let go of her resentments and find forgiveness.

An apology acknowledges
unconditional responsibility for
your mistake and a commitment
to do something about it.

The length of time required to
heal a hurt tends to go hand in
hand with how long ago the
mistake was made.

When a woman complains about the little stuff, a man assumes she is not appreciating the big stuff.

♥

'When he gives solutions instead of listening, it's not that he doesn't care, but he has forgotten what I need.'

Taking the necessary time to forgive and heal can result in a much better relationship.

If you can laugh and joke about situations that once would initiate an argument, your relationship can dramatically improve.

To forgive strengthens our love. Without forgiveness we cannot grow in love. In a sense it exercises our love and makes us stronger.

Our unresolved feelings are like a shadow: they don't go away when we leave town.

By doing too much, a woman loses touch with herself and her own needs.

If you feel self-assured, you won't feel like a victim at the whim of your partner's changing feelings.

Men respond much better when they are not seen as the problem but as the solution.

♥

Be gentle when you offer to help a man solve a problem, otherwise he will feel you think he doesn't have the competence to do it himself.

From the time they are little girls, women are taught to be desirable and not to desire.

Use negative beliefs as a flashlight to discover the unresolved feelings hidden in the closet of our unconscious.

By weathering the storms and droughts of love that inevitably arise from time to time, by repeatedly overcoming the challenge of harmonising differences, and by coming back to your commitment to having a quality relationship, you will find your soul mate and live happily ever after.

Trust is essential for a woman to continue getting turned on by her partner.

Men can speed up their healing process by hearing from others who are in pain, while women particularly benefit from being heard.

Real and lasting romance does
not require perfection.

To open our hearts, we
must be careful to counteract our
past personal conditioning and
fully experience each of the four
healing emotions: anger, sadness,
fear and sorrow.

Much of the time, ninety per
cent of the hurt we feel in present
time has to do with our past and
only ten per cent has to do with
what we think we are upset about.

♥

When a woman craves a man's
softness, it really is her own
softness that she is seeking to find.

Healing the heart is a
gradual process of unfoldment,
one layer at a time.

By linking the pain you feel in
the present with past pain, you
can most effectively release any
past repressed feelings that are
limiting your ability to feel and
release pain in the present.

Healing past feelings
strengthens our ability to forgive,
give thanks, and trust in
present time.

Whenever you experience
pain in the present, you will get
additional support by exploring
your past positive experiences.

One of a woman's biggest
obstacles to doing less
is that she doesn't know
how to say no lovingly.

Wanting more only
becomes a problem when what
we were expecting and wanting is
impossible and unrealistic.

By taking time to link your
present pain with the pain of
your past, you will be able to find
immediate relief and heal
your heart.

It is not the big things
that keep a relationship from
working, it is the little things.

Our ability to feel our emotions
is not based on gender difference.
Instead, this ability is greatly influenced
by our parents, society and early
childhood experiences.

A man can create enormous
pressure to measure up to his
own unrealistic standards.

If you busy yourself in the
process of parenting, you can
easily suppress your needs for
intimacy and love.

♥

When a man senses that he
can solve a problem, then he will
feel the energy to stay with it
until it is done.

Couples may get caught up fighting about the big things, but it is really the successful delivery of the little things that allows a woman to give the man the love he needs to keep giving of himself.

The alchemy of creating a loving relationship is a very delicate balance of give and take.

After years of learning
to put on emotional make-up to
be more desirable, a woman
becomes so good at covering up
that sometimes she fools herself
as well.

Without a clear understanding
of an alternative way of dealing
with his pain, a man will not
reach out for support.

Although making sacrifices is part of a relationship, many women make too many.

Without an understanding of the importance of making romantic gestures, a man will unknowingly stop doing the very things that made him so attractive in the beginning.

It is easy to be loving when you are in a good mood. The real test of love is to be loving even when you are in a bad mood.

The more a man apologises and is forgiven, the more considerate he becomes.

When a man experiences
intimacy, he may, periodically,
need to pull away before he
can get closer.

♥

Quite often, a man feels his
love when he is directly faced
with the possibility of losing a
woman.

Ultimately, a man is most attracted to a woman when she makes him feel masculine.

Women today experience a deep longing to feel the intimate passion that only good communication and romance can provide.

Needing more is not a turnoff,
but not appreciating it is.

♥

The more self-sufficient a
woman becomes, the more she
hungers for the nurturing
support of a man's romantic
affections, friendship and
companionship.

Modern women have become so
responsible for themselves that it
is no longer obvious why they
need a man.

To find forgiveness a woman
needs to talk about her feelings
until she feels that the man
understands why she is upset.

A woman does not have to be
helpless to ask a man for help,
nor does she have to be helpless
to need his support.

Trying new things actually gives
you more energy and makes you
more attractive.

There is no greater mistake
than to stop your life for a man.

♥

On the foundation that certain
issues are inevitable, a man can
begin to recognise that the
frustration he experiences has
more to do with his approach
than the woman he picks.

What men need most is to release their focus on doing the big things and focus more on the little things.

A man's greatest challenge is to put his best foot forward when his efforts have not been appreciated in the past.

When men and women misunderstand each other, misinterpret each other's actions, and miscommunicate their feelings, they are unable to successfully nurture each other and get what they need.

Real love is learning to love a real person with all their flaws and differences.

Deep inside, if some part
of a man feels hurt, rejected, or
inadequate, as he gets closer to a
woman these feelings will begin
to surface.

When resentment is released
with better communication,
understanding and forgiveness,
our differences do not show up
as obstacles.

A man needs to realise that he can seek to please a woman without taking responsibility for her happiness.

In a good relationship, couples work through their challenges and end up getting closer. They are able to look back and laugh about their frustrations and disappointments.

STARTING AGAIN

How do you know if you should try again? No one can answer that question for you; you must listen to your loving heart.

♥

To successfully share with another, we must heal our neediness and have a strong sense of self.

Be careful not to repress
feelings, because they can cause
self-destructive tendencies.

If you are starting over, feel
confident that you will find the
love you deserve. You can be
inspired to share the special love
you feel deep in your heart.

If you are able to nurture the healing of a broken heart, it also will grow back stronger.

♥

Each time you follow your feelings of attraction and then, after you get to know the person, that person goes away, you are actually preparing yourself to be attracted to the right one.

When the pain in our hearts
is healed we are left with loving
memories and peace.

The very act of saying no to a
relationship that is not right for
you fine-tunes your ability to be
attracted to the person who is
right for you.

It is impossible for your heart
to open fully to another when it
is completely closed to someone
in your past.

Right after a break-up and
before getting involved again,
it is important for a man to
regain once more his sense of
independence, self-sufficiency
and autonomy.

To heal our hurt we must
feel it, but also recognise that it
belongs to our past.

♥

We can create the right healing
attitude to heal our hearts by
taking time to explore our past
feelings and to enrich them with
the intent to find forgiveness,
increase our understanding,
give thanks and trust again.

Remember that the dawn
of a new day comes after the
darkest moment of the night.
Things may get darker but the
light of love and relief
will come.

Taking time to heal our hearts
is a powerful way to boost our
self-esteem.

With an open heart, our soul
will guide us as to whether to
continue the relationship
or to break up.

Each time you follow your heart
and then recognise that someone
is not right for you, then you are
one step closer to finding the
right person for you.

The time you spend in any
relationship is not a loss if you
learn from it and complete it
in a positive way.

The difference between success
and failure is being able to learn
from our mistakes to become
more discerning.

When a relationship ends,
it is good to take some time to
reflect on the gift and then begin
again. When you feel grateful for
something, then you are ready
to move on.

The way we cope with the
loss of love reveals how we may
automatically cope with love
in the future.

When a relationship ends,
it is good to take some time to
reflect on the gift and then begin
again. When you feel grateful for
something, then you are ready
to move on.

The way we cope with the
loss of love reveals how we may
automatically cope with love
in the future.

Strong, independent, assertive
and successful women often have
difficulty in finding the right man
and then sustaining a relationship,
primarily because the very
characteristics that make them
successful at work can make them
unsuccessful in relationships.

❤

Good endings make
good beginnings.

Strong, independent, assertive and successful women often have difficulty in finding the right man and then sustaining a relationship, primarily because the very characteristics that make them successful at work can make them unsuccessful in relationships.

Good endings make good beginnings.